TRACK & TRACE

TRACK & TRACE
ZACHARIAH WELLS

DESIGNED & DECORATED
BY SETH

BIBLIOASIS

*for my mother
and for my father*

And everybody hoped to leave some trace. What did I mean by that? Had she ever observed those new aeroplanes which flew at colossal altitudes? They pass, they disappear, but they leave a white trail in the sky when they are gone. That was a trace. Or a person crosses a snowfield and disappears. There's no one anywhere, only snow, a wide empty plain, but then a wanderer who's lost his way comes along, and what does he find? Right, a track.

—Ivan Klíma

Green air and a rusty babble.
Tender tight fists of fiddleheads
fronding into bitter-leafed ferns.
Salamanders, nude under turned-
over stones, and slugs, creeping beads
of cool snot. Foam of bubbles

coating a dam of fallen tree rubble.
Cicadas scraping shrill creeds
and credentials. Flowers where a fire once burned.
Brown blurred pheasants churning
green air. His last full head
of hair and the first faint traces of stubble.

DREAM VISION OF THE FLOOD

I must build this house, I must
build this house high on the hill
on borrowed cash, I must build it
now, bring with me all books
worth saving: I dreamed the end
last night, dreamed this three-countied

Island's borders redrawn
by water, green archipelagos of stranded
holsteins on high ground, lowing at insidious
inundation, the mainland bridge
a beheaded, bobtailed leviathan arched
in Northumberland, whose waters, with the Gulf's,

engorged oxbowed rivers, glutted
ponds into rust-red lakes, filled our hardwrought
valley, a tub with plugged drains,
slowly, while we molded contours of mud, heaping
wet red earth like the swallows under our eaves,
in vain—only the chimneys left when it settled,

perches for cormorants drying spread wings in the sun.

THE POND

for Andy

The pond was first a creek,
percolating into a reek-
rich bog. Then came dumptrucks
and dozers, to heap shale and rock
across the creek's
path and pack
it tight, a pale blue PVC pipe stuck
into the dyke
like a periscope stack
to drain the eventual flood. Trickle
by drop the muddy tub filled. It took
six weeks.
A haphazard dock,
cobbled together with planks
and peeled cedar trunks
for pilings, was sunk
into red mud. Finally, the creeping flood broke
the overflow's rim to slake
the parched bed of the brook.
Once sediment settled down into the muck,
the waters cleared, it was time to take stock.
And so, the pond was stocked
with rainbows raised in a tank,

but their ranks
shrank
and shrank.
I caught the last one, his once-iridescent flank
blotched and pocked
by fungus and wounds, stubborn underslung jaw hooked
up like a gaff.
                Still, the pond teems, surface pinked
by local speckled,
rising to flies in the dusk
as I watch from my spot on the rot-patched dock.

CORMORANT

I

From the dock I watched it circle slow, drop
lower, flare, then plop onto the pond's calm
water: this cormorant, crow duck, sea raven;
this lawyer, nigger goose, shag; this devil

in life's tree devouring time, this hook-beaked
black archaic bolt of snake-necked fish-death;
this haunter of powerlines, tideflats, beaches,
wharves—perched on stakes, wet sable wings spread

like a fabulous cape—this one left its castle
of sticks and shit to hassle tame trout.
I knew Father would want it out; he forgave
no trespassers poaching his stock, had even,

with a neighbour's shotgun, brought down
a Great Blue, tied its carcass high in the tall pine
by the pond, a lesson to would-be
intruders to bypass what they can't

well swallow. (The trout, see, were more
than the heron's gullet could handle, too much
for its instincts and eyes to resist, so
the gormless bird, stilted in shallows, scissor-

speared rainbows and left their corpses to bloat.)
When the heron started to stink and rot
up there on its conifer cross, Father cut it down,
buried the withered king in the garden.

II

To shoo the intruder from our shores,
I went in to Father's shop and got the Crossman
off its hook. Back on the dock, butt shoulder-
squared, sights aligned, I plunked the dumb thing

in the rump. It half-lifted, water-walked
and spread its herald wings—then didn't fly,
but dove into the teeming trouthouse, popped
up at the pond's far end. I shot and shot

again, I nagged that damn shag from one
end of the slough to the other, but the bird
preferred water's wet shelter to the open sky.
Father came out grim-faced, launched our tin

canoe and shoved off. Each time
he drew near, the lawyer did its diving act.
He beached the boat, his face blotched red,
blue eyes flashing death. Shoot the goddamn thing,

he said. I fired a shot smack in its breast—
it subbed again. Father grabbed the rifle,
loaded, cocked, took aim, pulled, and caught
the crooked neck. The head jerked down, the body

bobbed. With his paddle blade, Father scooped
the floating shroud. It puked mustard stuff, guano
streamed from its anus. Bile rose
in my throat, I choked—and I swallowed.

RHYTHM

burlap sacks of shorn wool, pungent
cushions in the porch on which

to perch and tie a boot, until,
unstuffed, soaked in the tub, hung up,

carded into batts, pinched and twisted
on the bobbin to the treadle's

metric creaking, wound up in skeins
and clews, strung through heddles

and levered by pedals to let
pass the shooshing shuttle through

the warp to form a weft—or purled
and knitted into patterns, into

socks and toques and mittens, scarves
and gloves and sweaters, to the metric

clicking of the needles as my
mother counted stitches in a row

BRIAR PATCH

Sticky wicket, Brer Rabbit's deliverance,
that crazy cane thicket, more than head high,
held mysteries infinite, terrors, delights.
Only sunlight pierced its intricate

barbed matrix—so seemed it, but we plied paths
of bent, rent, trampledown stems, small-bodied
maze of cross-hatching raspberry gathering
tracks. At the heart thrummed a grey paper

hive. Yellowjackets squeezed from and sucked in
to its tip, briar patch hum cum prime hazard,
what all the buzz was about. Though nervous,
we knew: be deftly deferent pickers

and ye be spared stings—a scratch the sole hurt
suffered. One fall Father John-Deered the patch
under: "What a muddle—best to start fresh."
That said, he set a match to cane stubble.

FOOL'S ERRAND

My mother sent me into the swirling
bowl of stirred-up curdled milk
our valley was, wild with wind and skirling
snow that fastened onto lashes, there to melt
and bead and break mute light, unfurling
bows like multicoloured scraps of silk.

Bring them in, she said, they'll freeze to death
out there. Out there then I went,
tripping through the hip-high snow, each breath
a wet rag gasp, as weaving wind sent
shuttling snow between my teeth and hooked a snowdrop wreath
around my neck. When I found them, he was bent

over her back, his forepaws clutched her rump.
I tried hard to pull him out of her,
but still he blindly pumped and pumped,
eyes shut against the storm that heaped snow in his fur.
I hauled off and handed him one solid thump
which only shook his haunches bare.

I stumbled home and left them there.

HE LEARNS FAITH IN HIS INSTINCTS

In practice, I'd shag flyballs
till well past dusk, the contrast
between ball and sky growing dimmer
and dimmer as white and blue bled
into twilight, till I quit
doing it so much by sight, let
guess and instinct guide my feet
to where I thought the ball
would be, to where the crack
of it leaving the bat
said it should land,
stretch out my glove-hand,
listen for the sound-glimmer
of leather thunking firmly into well-worked leather.

THE OLD GREY MARE

Finicky fuckin thing that old silver Ford—clutch
so touchy no one could start er 'thout stallin
least once. And gutless! Christ, that clunkety four-
banger couldn't climb nothin without gearin down—

burnt out three clutches pullin stuck neighbours
from ditches. Didn't help none when the old man,
comin home from the Shore, nodded and pitched off
the road, a quarter mile shy of our drive.

Must've tramped the gas when he passed out, hit
the ditch like a ramp: stripped bark from a birch
nine feet off the ground, woke up, unbuckled, lurched
down the dark empty road home, a cage full o cracked

ribs. Bought the wroteoff wreck off the broker,
got er fixed up with parts offa other old trucks.
New silver paint was a different batch, tho, not quite
a match—no, never was the same, after that.

BACKROADS

Roads like seams between swatches of green
Roads speckled with worm-lousy apples
Roads like a lattice laid flat on the lawn
Roads with ditchfuls of lupins and bottles

Roads sprouting chanterelles in the shade of their shoulders
Roads lined on Sunday with pickups and cars
Roads over hills and passing through polders
Roads like dendrites, arteries, scars

Roads of snow crisscrossed by fox-tracks and hare
Roads for the consummation of lust
Roads leading nowhere
Roads kicking up billows of dust

Roads ruddled, riddled and rutted
Roads trudged down like the Way of the Cross
Roads through towns abandoned and gutted
Derelict roads gone to alders and moss

HE FINDS AN ACCEPTABLE WAY TO GRIEVE

The day my dog Mutt lay down and died
of old age by the stream bank, I was obliged
to work a shift at the ice-cream store
at Cavendish beach. Since I had no more
than a dead dog for excuse, I went to work
on time (stupid ethics wouldn't let me shirk
my duty to co-workers and employer just to mourn
a favourite pet; such things must be borne
with grace, or so I thought)—but I couldn't face
the endless pace of sunburnt tourists placing
impatient orders for pralines, vanilla, hot fudge,
peanuts. I found a place I wouldn't have to budge
from, but still could earn my keep: in the corner
of the store, a waffle iron with three burners
on which we cooked our cones, a job no one wanted
for long (that spot was hot as a sauna,
and no matter how nimble your fingers, bound
to inflict the odd burn—we all had wounds
from that hellish contraption), but I stayed there all shift,
with my back to the steady drift
of customers, facing the blank wall
of gleaming white tiles, breathing the cloying pall

of batter, rolling cone after cone after cone
in the stainless steel mold, alive and alone.
In the midst of all the chaos and clatter
the cones were all that mattered
to me: lay them out in neat rows
on their racks, make verse of prose
fact, stack them in piles six high,
stow them in the cupboard to cool off and dry,
then start again—I made at least a thousand cones,
while my mother covered Mutt with a cairn of red stones.

THE STRANGER

Without a thought for how she'd feel,
he lit out on the road once more
on two wheels bolted to a steel-
tubed frame, twin cylinders, wide-bored,

hammered by a harnessed fire,
unrolled an asphalt belt beneath
night's black starstudded treadless tire.
A purring motor underneath

his crotch and buttocks did far more
for him than any lover's heaving
flesh and dampened skin. The back door
was his favourite way of leaving

once the deed was done. Moving on
was his forte and moving fast
across the land what he loved best—
see trees give way to plains and on

to lakes and deserts, mountains, seas,
all the varied haunts of human
life—suburbs, trailer parks and cities—
the houses where men and women

bickered, loved and slept together.
He was more transient than weather;
no sooner would he stop to rest
and get his bearings, he'd get restive

again, climb back in the saddle,
flick the spring-loaded kickstand back,
twist his right wrist up, skedaddle
down another unknown track.

Leaving all of this stuff behind
meant more to him than land, than bread,
than fame. In his strange nomad mind,
it was grooves worn in the roadbed

that seemed to be his home instead.

after Rilke

AT THE REBECCA COHN AUDITORIUM

I am listening
I am listening to Al Purdy at the Rebecca Cohn
in underground sunlight
and you can tell that I am a sensitive man
And I notice that Purdy is a sensitive man too
as he reads a poem that says so
However jokily, I see it's true
And he reads other poems as well
poems about beer and fights with his wife
and things I understand
such as the Arctic
for I have been there
and I am a sensitive man
I have been to Pangnirtung
where I saw the ground willow
rooted stubbornly in its rocky bed
I have seen the delicate things
carved from serpentine by toothless old men
and I have seen noisy flowers
which I would bottle and press
as "small yellow shouts"
Okay, so those were poppies and saxifrage
and not "Arctic rhododendrons"
but the point is that I am a sensitive man
and what Al is saying, I dig
and I dig the big resonant voice
improbably emanating from that long lanky frame
topped by a mop of straight white hair

and I think to myself
Jeez, maybe I should write flower poems
But the North I know is not the same
as the place Purdy briefly toured in '65
There are more white people for instance
and more machines
and I am both of them
There is cable TV, cellphones
mansions on the hill over Frobisher Bay
Stone carvings get shipped by the planeload
from Cape Dorset to Montreal
on jets that thunder down Iqaluit's 9000 paved feet
and those carvings are shaped
not by handmade tools
but with Dremels and sanders and drills
and when I go up to Al
at the end of the night
so he can sign the copy of his book I just bought
I see that he is a very tired old man
and I am sad
for at least one ivory thought
is about to grow cold

MUSSEL MUD

The sudden stink of mussel mud drifting
through the warehouse doors, blown off the bay
on the south shore of this northern island, lifted
me up and led me like Ariadne's thread
through a synaptic matrix of daedals
till I landed, a boy, on the north shore
of a southern island, that fertile pong
in my nostrils, breeze tangling my hair,
seabirds shrieking their raucous diphthongs—
then, from the cloudless sky, a man spoke
and I woke from my dream and I was here,
in a warehouse choked with diesel smoke,
the familiar reek gone from the air.

NIMBLE & POISE

A jack caulking high in a maple hacks down
a century's growth, lopping off autumn-
tinged limbs and letting them freefall,
flutter, to earth, to concrete, to asphalt,
chunks of trunk thunking like dud munitions.
His sputtering saw spits out scintillas
of chips, glittering in October sun,
sawdust seed scattered over Esplanade.

Buckled to the dwindling titan, pinned
to a spartan blue backdrop, this urban
feller is essence of nimble and poise,
his movements tuned to the vulgar noise
of a full-throttle two-stroke, amber-clad
branchflares dropping like brands to the ground.

KADDISH

I'm told that I resemble you. I do,
it's true, like an Arab a Jew, I can see

me in you, right to my left shoe, bootstrapped
and blue. Dear zeyda, dear grampa, dear Lou,

let's marry, let's say our I do's, our boo-
hoos, our adieus. She never left you—you

were threaded in her like a screw, staining
her like a tattoo, drubbing and draining

her blue. It was you, Lou, you who flew,
old Lear, into rages and bottles and fugues,

into the storm you flew—where I met you,
cursing the gods and the fools who weren't you.

Goddamnit, grandfather, I am you,
stubborn, wicked and true. I never knew

you in life, but I didn't need to.

STEADY

Ted, forgive me, if you haven't already.
Our neuroses failed to dovetail those years,
my manic benders mismatched to your steady
swallows of bourbon. Neuroses? No, fears,
old friend, if we're going to be honest,
our fears of growing older and going
nowhere. Me, I went nowhere often,
relinquished my blood and bones to No One,
who you saw in my eyes as I sat on your john
hauling away at a straitlaced boot,
muttering curses in a Babylon
of tongues. Our friendship froze down to the root.
Forgive me, Ted, if you haven't already.
Take my hand. Shake it. It's steady.

FIELD OF FLOES

for R.

Here we are on the Island's northern tip.
A black and yellow checkered road sign stuck
in the frozen ground hard by the crumbling lip
of the cliff warns that we can take our truck
no further. As if we needed telling:
before us, the Gulf spread out, resplendent,
white and crystal blue, a blank abundant
field of floes, heaved, humped and swelling
over each slow tidal wave. The wind's fierce,
love. This is the first you've seen a solid
ocean? Yes, it happens here most years.
We could step across to other islands,
no matter what the sign says. We could go
and get lost in the million acre flow.

DOE

To our eyes, she escaped
the sheer scarp's face,
minced across pebbles,
high-stepped over stones,
dainty dame, down to the wet

rocks, where in a graceful
squat, she pissed: a silhouette
shudder, unaware of our presence,
tail a slight swish; against
the backdrop of the Basin's

sun-struck escutcheon,
a motive blot, then
a breeze traitored our scents
and she bolted, that flash
of white tail a beacon.

AFTER THE BLIZZARD

I

Staring out at the empty parking lot
buried, I can't but be tempted to think:
Blank page. Clotted cream. White sheet without blot
of blood upon it. That won't do. I shrink
from clean metaphor. One block down, I know
the suburbs' urgent traffic crawls and clogs
this coast town's constricted veins, greasy snow
humped grey anent trenches, slush-crumby cogs
grinding in a seized economy's engine.
The liquor store enjoys a roaring trade;
socked-in folks stock up needful stuff again,
unimpressed by this trick that winter's played.

In curfewed dark, the amber beacon of a plow
strobes the first flakes of another night's snow.

II

Strobes. The furred flakes of another night's snow
garnish metre-deep heaps that are being
shoved, shovelled, lugged, bypassed, cussed at and blown
all over Halifax; dogs are peeing
in it; dumptrucks haul enormous sullied
dollops dockwards to nourish the harbour.
(Dispensation's been granted to muddy
our common latrine.)
                              Over my neighbour's
fence, I launch blocks that I've carved from the drifts,
shirking the work of a far longer trek—
and pay for this lazy sin: fine stuff sifts,
settles wet on the white skin of my neck.

Shoulders squinched, I focus up through a squint:
crows quarter five-fingered wings against wind.

III

Crows quarter five-fingered wings against wind
and dip and wheel and rip and skate like kites
without strings, sheer at each other, brake, bend
off, a feather from wrecking their dogfights.

Some claim that brute beasts have no sense of fun—
that's dumb. A few make the most of unplanned
time off, don snowshoes and skis, sled and run
through ultra-urbane winter wonderland;

others maunder in gloom cursing profit
lost, crunching the cost of this weatherbomb;
and one bone-weary poet pens sonnets
to celebrate an exceptional storm.

Image-sick, he seeks moral straws to clutch
at—Yes! Most of what is done is too much.

IV

What? Yes: most of what is done *is* too much.
God, when there are so many things not begun—
rosebuds to gather, pied beauties to touch
with eyes, ears, nose, teeth, toes, fingers and tongue;

strange lands to visit and spices to taste;
heights still unfathomed, depths yet to be climbed;
blank pages to fill, red lips to be kissed;
beds and books unbroken, words left unrhymed—

why do we persist in boring ourselves?
When life's a great multifarious feast,
why do we storehouse canned goods on our shelves?
How to account for such thrift-conscious waste?

When life's a hundred thousand times too short,
why do we settle for scrap, shred, crumb, ort?

V

Weather settles. Hoary scraps, shreds, crumbs, orts
of crumbly snow turned concrete in the cold
and salt-pocked hardpack sparkle like borts
strewn in walkways carved in spall-etched frost-walled
Maginot trenches, treacherous goatpath
networks, navigable to the nimble
alone—work's halted as though the sabbath
compelled it. The fittest now must stumble
clumsy while the housebound haunt bay windows,
waiting on zephyr's tepid breath to melt
impediments, in fear of glissandos
into broken coccyx, hip, elbow dealt
by glib ice on asphalt: a mean hard card
and shortcut to a frost-hummocked boneyard.

VI

A shortcut through the frost-hummocked boneyard
should have brought the drunk poet home sooner,
but for faux pas and foxholes, our stoned bard
made unsteady progress.
                              (Was it moon or
streetlight that dusted the scene so ghastly?
Or was it that last half-pint of cider
that limned a blanched tableau like some lost Li
Po poem?)
                  He broke like a Dave Stieb slider,
or like the sun rising, through the wrought east
gate of the dead's condominium
                                        —and there
a loader bulled elegant on fraught greased
axles, scooping buckets of crud. Stand there
was all he'd manage, transfixed by the diesel
dance
            —and the driver like Munch at his easel.

VII

I dance and shiver like Munch at his easel
straining to expel this Norwegian cold
from fingers and toes: our heat has fizzled
out, our furnace drained of fuel, the old-
school moulded space heaters radiate nothing.
Ironclad hibernation. Studious
Cavern.
              Chilblained bum, I layer clothing.
My neighbour's chimneypot spouts sooty O's—
O, I covet fossil-fired comfort and curse
my landlord's neglect. That dumb fuck'll rue
forgetting to top up the tank.
                                    Of course
I'm sheer bluff: bowser truck'll be here soon.

In wait, I wander and get lost in thought,
staring out at the empty parking lot.

SPEND TIME IN NOVA SCOTIA;
YOUR SOUL WILL THANK YOU.

Under white high-wattage sodium glare,
Under clocks' inaudible *tick-tack-tock*,
The folding folders stand and fold
And chuck flyers in bins with a *thok*.

In the fibreglass, I-beam-ribbed hold
Of a warehouse, blinking folders shuffle
Soles across concrete, suffer and shuffle
And fold, amid whacks of stacked pallets,

Catalogues, pamphlets, clackety racket
Of tabbers tab-tabbing, belts whirring, backs
Creaking and cracking—red-eyed they stare,
No longer seeing the sun-kissed vistas

Backdropping blissed-out couples of tourists
Redeeming profit and loss at the beach
Round the bend, blank-faced and burning
Under high-wattage heatlamps of heaven.

SLUGS

Leaning into the trash box out back—
all those garbage days forgotten
or passed over due to sloth—
I hauled up moldered slabs of rotten
boxes, reeking wrack
of plastic sacks and scraps of cloth,
and unwrapped
twelve monstrous spotted slugs.
Some pardic cross
of cunts and cocks,
they slimed there in the sludge;
stretched out long,
then squished compact,
they scudged around the box's bottom,
crossed paths in an erotic splay
(no earthly act
so slow and solemn
as slug-on-slug foreplay)
while others humped
motherly their spineless shlong
bodies across
glister-lumped
clusters of eggs—and one
began a sluggish crawl
up the box's wooden wall,
trailing after a glistening track,

till halfway up it poked
its head-end through the gap
between two slats
and paused there—
seemed to soak
the world in through its feelers,
wriggling in the air—
then out it squeezed
like the bored striptease
of roadside tavern peelers.
It spent a steep minute in the sun—
and turned back,
back through the crack,
back with its fellows in the wet warm vault.
It stiffened with that lot
in a shower of salt.

OUT

Out with the garbage, the fag ends, the clutter
Out with the eaten, the worn down, the odd
Out with the beaten, the shuffle and sputter
Of words half unspoken and feet poorly shod

Out with the photos, the journals, the clippings
Out with the fucked-up, the fucked-out, the dead
Out with the drivel, the dribble and drippings
Out with the starving and out with the fed

Out with the baby, the bathtub, the water
Out with the lambkin and out with the kid
Out with the innocent, out with the slaughter
Out with the bum, the rummy, the skid

Out with the shit-stained, the ruined, the wasted
Out with the shot and the clubbed and the shivved
Out with the pinned-up, the plastered, the pasted
Out with the landfill of a life half-lived

So much reflected, so much exposed, in façades
of glass ringing this cobbled courtyard
built on fill. This Creek not merely False,
but dammed, dyked, walled,
cranes opposite intent on concrete erector
sets, booms indexed to a boom in the sector,
also false, fuelled by empty
specs and green dreams of Olympian
gold.
      Once, rats scrabbled in the rattle-trap shacks
and sheds they shared with schizo skids and whacked-
out addicts.
              And once, a limb washed
ashore, saltchuck sloshing
in the boot it still wore, unclaimed
by any owner.
              Cute? No. This place is maimed.

HERON, FALSE CREEK

There, Heron, you stand
in my shadow, stick pegs
and twigged feet steeped
in the freezing Creek's

shallows, scissor-beaked
slink neck stapled
to a feathered bundle.
There, Heron, you stand,

avatar of angler's
waiting, waiting, calm
as monks praying, steeped
in the shitty Creek's

tide-drained stink—
then tensile—blink—
like a Singer's
stainless needle,

that scissor beak
stabs the reeking
Creek, springs back
with silver, flipping,

flashing in the seawall
lamp standard's
glare. With a slurp
and a shake, like

a puffy glutton
at Monk's Oyster Bar
(stilted in False Creek's
salted shallows)

sucking a shucked mollusc
from its crusted
shell, you swallow,
Heron, stand there

in my shadow, stare
up at the seawall,
skronk, and awkwardly
flop up into the air.

A WINTER

It was a winter of atmospheric depressions
It was a winter of anhedonic ennui
It was a winter of dumb indecision
It was a winter of her, a winter of me

It was a winter of silt in the Fraser
It was a winter of tugboats and freight trains
It was a winter of rust on the razor
It was a winter of nightmares and rain

It was a winter of dull unemployment
It was a winter of landlords and in-laws
It was a winter of ill-planned deployments
It was a winter of hammers and saws

It was a winter of wrongheaded answers
It was a winter in which nothing clicked
It was the winter the cat died of cancer
It was the winter you quickened and kicked

THERE IS SOMETHING INTRACTABLE IN ME

Keeping me from sentimental verse
About your birth and growth and milestones.
Love like this is best left mute, though I curse
Each impulse to speak, catching like bones
Blockading my throat. Can't say what's worse:

Diving in headfirst or standing shin-deep
On a shoal. Never been much of a swimmer.
Vigils, my son, I've held, to see you sleep
In dusk-dim light and I've felt the dimmer
Numbness in me melt. I've tried to keep

Watch from a safe ascetic distance,
Emotion held in check—a trick that's killed
Love in the past. The slant consonance
Linking us will stall me, until I've fulfilled,
Stubbornly, the demands of these constraints.

GOING FORWARD

Your ambition puts me to shame,
little man: the constant forward
drive despite the pegleg lame-
duck scuffle of your awkward

proto-crawl. And look at me:
unshaven, unemployed and slack,
going nowhere, pushing thirty-three
like a shopping cart heaped with sacks

of cans and bottles. No one'd blink
if all you did was sleep and shit
and smile, but you squirm like a skink,
scoot off in pursuit of that bit

of paper or plastic or fluff
in the corner—which I've neglected
to sweep up, stuck here on my duff.
Next thing, you'll be elected

class president, voted most likely
to go places. I'll be at home,
contemplating the unlikely
prospects of writing a poem.

PRESS

I once preferred a keen and perfect
cutting edge, a right-angled sheet trimmed neat
with borders that might snick an errant

fingertip. I later played it safer, seeking
corners that were curved or bevel, the better
to deflect attack, embraces and attention.

My predilection now is for the deckled
indents of a homemade page, fibre-flecked
and textured like a slept-in bed dented

from the press of its residents, a set
of lovers well fitted to each other's
folding flaws, growing more attached each week

as they fade and sag and grey together.

THE SAME MAN NEVER STEPS INTO A RIVER TWICE

Find yourself a flat stone by the bank,
sit down and watch the river purl and froth
and flow. Note where it pools and how its flanks
straighten and bend into bows. It is both

protean and permanent. You'll never
see the same wave twice; the molecules
of H_2O won't sit still and make fools
of sages who would fix them. But clever

man has done it, naming this forever
fitful stream of fluxity, nailing its
matrix, *water*, and its channel, *river*,
as if they were as still as stone. A man sits

by a river. He is no more the same
man he was, yet he bears a constant name.

after Jean-Baptiste Chassignet

ORKNEY REPORT

Everything here's impossibly old
and once you've seen one ruinous cottage

or roofless church, you're better off
breaking the spine of a book at the noust

than carrying on with the tour. It should
be said, though, that a crumbling broch

is far finer than abandoned brick-
n-mortar batteries, Brodgar boggles

the brain, and it must be something
else to see the solstice sun flicker

and ripple on the rear wall of Maeshowe—
but sure as this landmass drifted

from Orcadie, it'll all wind up
in the sea. Five millennia back,

the waves that buss the buttressed seawall
at Skara Brae were half a mile of dunes

away. The Old Man of Hoy's a peedie boy
compared with what's crumpled about him.

Across Scapa Flow, the Flotta flare
burns all roofless day without blinking.

WATER WORKS

Forty-some paces into the Gulf
you'll find the work of forty-odd years:
rings of rock that once cased cottage wells
where dwellers drew fresh water, sunk now
in the salt swell and swum around
by fishes. We get smaller year by
year. The breaks we build to brake our shrinkage—
riprap and seawalls, baskets of stone—
only make things worse: they make the patient
ocean more resourceful. Gone Panmure
Island's marram-anchored dunes. Gone the wharves
of Basin Head. Gone the elephant-
shaped rock whose feet we shod in concrete
to keep him for the tourists.

THE POETRY IN HIM

The poetry in him's not hard to miss—
Lear's Kent, steady servant, taking cover
when cynics stormed the stage, but never
hiding out. No lies in him, his honest
talk not florid, stripped of artifice
and ornament. Plain. Don't take his silence
for indifference, don't mistake it for a lack
of love, nor his boxer's skill for violence,
his aptitude with axe and saw and maul
for bloodlust. Flawed? Yes, but what he hacked
apart he raised into a home, a small
solid shield against impending weather,
and at its heart a Jøtul blazing hot.
My father was not a man who said a lot.

SKUNK

The dim stink of skunk carried in
from the woods isn't unpleasant—
distance and diffusion
make it more perfume than weapon

and it mingles in the brainpan
with a memory you can't put a finger on
but linger over anyway—a vaccine
couldn't be, without a speck of infection;

anti-venom is drawn from pure poison;
and the life you lead on this land
was allowed by the death of your parents.
It hurt, but diffusion and distance

make it bearable. When you live with a constant
scent in your nostrils, you can't
stand it at first, then come to love it, then
it grows so faint you forget its existence.

ACKNOWLEDGEMENTS

Versions of some of these poems, sometimes under different titles, have
appeared in the following:

Journals

Canadian Notes & Queries:	"Doe" "Water Works" "Out" "Press"
The Danforth Review:	"Mussel Mud"
Elysian Fields Quarterly (US):	"He Learns Faith in His Instincts"
Event:	"Field of Floes" "Skunk" "Steady"
The Fiddlehead:	"Corona: After the Blizzard"
The New Quarterly:	"He Finds an Acceptable Way to Grieve" "Nimble & Poise" "The Pond"
Rhythm Poetry Magazine:	"Kaddish" "The Poetry in Him" "The Same Man Never Steps into a River Twice" "There Is Something Intractable in Me"
Riddle Fence:	"Rhythm"

Anthologies

In Fine Form:	"Fool's Errand"
And Left a Place to Stand On:	"At the Rebecca Cohn Auditorium" "Mussel Mud"
Rocksalt:	"Heron, False Creek"
A Verse Map of Vancouver:	"Leg-in-Boot Square"

Websites

The Afterword (*National Post* blog):	"Going Forward"
Canadian Poets:	"Corona: After the Blizzard" "Fool's Errand"
P.E.I. Poet Laureate's Site:	"Field of Floes" (Audio) "Skunk"
Seen Reading:	"A Winter" (Audio)

Chapbooks

After the Blizzard
Littlefishcart Press, 2008: "After the Blizzard"

Fool's Errand
Saturday Morning Chapbooks,
2004: "Briar Patch"
"Cormorant"
"Dream Vision of the Flood"
"Fool's Errand"
"The Old Grey Mare"
"What He Found Growing in the Woods"

Ludicrous Parole
Mercutio Press, 2005: "The Stranger"

Books

Unsettled
Insomniac Press, 2004: "Mussel Mud"

The author acknowledges the support of the Canada Council for the Arts and the Nova Scotia Department of Tourism, Culture and Heritage.

ABOUT THE AUTHOR

Zachariah Wells is the Reviews Editor for *Canadian Notes & Queries* and the author of *Unsettled*, a collection of poetry about Canada's Eastern Arctic, and *Anything But Hank!*, a verse story for children, co-written with Rachel Lebowitz and illustrated by Eric Orchard. He is also the editor of the anthology *Jailbreaks: 99 Canadian Sonnets*. Wells was born and raised on Prince Edward Island and has since lived in many parts of Canada, working in a variety of occupations in the transportation sector and as a freelance writer.

Contents

FIRST EDITION

Library and Archives Canada Cataloguing in Publication

Wells, Zachariah, 1976-
    Track & trace : poems / Zachariah Wells ; designed and illustrated by SETH.

ISBN 978-1-897231-58-6

    I. Seth, 1962- II. Title. III. Title: Track and trace.

PS8645 E458 T73 2009   C811'.6   C2009-904133-2

Edited by Carmine Starnino

Canada Council   Conseil des Arts
for the Arts   du Canada

Canadian   Patrimoine
Heritage   canadien

ONTARIO ARTS COUNCIL
CONSEIL DES ARTS DE L'ONTARIO

We gratefully acknowledge the support of the Canada Council for the Arts, Canadian Heritage, and the Ontario Arts Council for our publishing program.

PRINTED AND BOUND IN CANADA